cupcakes

cupcakes

Susannah Blake

photography by Martin Brigdale

RYLAND
PETERS
& SMALL

LONDON NEW YORK

First published in the United
Kingdom in 2007
by Ryland Peters & Small
20–21 Jockey's Fields
London WC1R 4BW
www.rylandpeters.com

20 19 18 17 16 15 14 13 12 11

ISBN: 978 1 84597 378 0

A CIP record for this book is
available from the British Library.
Printed and bound in China.

Notes

- All spoon measurements are
level, unless otherwise specified.
- All eggs are medium, unless
otherwise specified. Uncooked
or partly cooked eggs should not
be served to the very young, the
very old, those with compromised
immune systems or to pregnant
women.

Acknowledgements

For Fred, Eleanor and little Tomski.

Senior Designer Steve Painter
Commissioning Editor Julia Charles
Editor Rachel Lawrence
Production Gemma Moules
Art Director Anne-Marie Bulat
Publishing Director Alison Starling

Food Stylist Linda Tubby
Prop Stylist Helen Trent
Indexer Hilary Bird

contents

making cupcakes

So utterly cute that no grown adult can resist, cupcakes baked in pretty paper cases are the ultimate in feel-good confectionery. Whether decorated in pretty pastels with dainty sugar flowers or swirled with an indulgently rich, dark chocolate frosting, a plateful of cupcakes is sure to lift your spirits and bring a smile to your face.

You can eat them pretty much any time – mid-morning with a cup of coffee, with a cup of tea at 4 o'clock or after dinner instead of dessert. They're also great tucked into a lunchbox or in the middle of the night as a cure for those raging midnight munchies. Cupcakes make the perfect gift, too – nestled in a pretty box or basket for a special occasion, or simply taken on a plate to offer as a hostess gift.

The simplest cupcake mixture is made with an equal weight of butter, sugar, eggs and flour, beaten to a smooth, creamy consistency with a splash of milk, then spooned into paper cases and baked until risen and golden. To this basic mixture you can then add various flavourings, such as vanilla, lemon or chocolate.

basic cupcake recipe

115 g butter, at room temperature

115 g caster sugar

2 eggs

115 g self-raising flour

2 tablespoons milk

1 teaspoon vanilla extract, grated zest of 1 lemon or 2 tablespoons cocoa powder (optional)

a 12-hole muffin tin

makes 12

Preheat the oven to 180°C (350°F) Gas 4, then line the muffin tin with paper cases.

Beat the butter and sugar together in a bowl until pale and fluffy. You can do this either by hand, or using an electric mixer. Then beat in the eggs, one at a time.

Sift over the flour, then fold in by hand. Stir in the milk and flavouring (if using) to make a creamy, spoonable mixture.

Spoon heaped tablespoonfuls of the mixture into each paper case, then bake for about 17 minutes until risen and golden and a skewer inserted into the centre comes out clean.

Transfer the cakes to a wire rack and leave to cool completely before decorating.

decorating cupcakes

Most cakes can be made the day before and stored in an airtight container, but they're usually better decorated shortly before serving. There are literally hundreds of ways to decorate cupcakes, from a simple dusting of icing sugar to thick swirls of creamy frosting. You can also add an array of decorations and toppings, from glacé cherries or toasted nuts to intricate sugar decorations available from large supermarkets and specialist kitchen shops.

First of all, you need to decide whether you want elegant flat-topped cakes or cheeky domed ones. Domed cakes are ideal for thick and creamy frostings, such as cream cheese frosting or chocolate ganache, or you can spoon over a glacé or fondant icing and let it spread over the top.

Flat-topped cakes are well suited to fondant and glacé icings that can be spooned on top and left to settle into a glossy, smooth surface. For flat-topped cakes, put a little less cake mixture in each paper case, then carefully slice off the domed tops using a serrated knife once baked and cooled.

fondant icing

For domed cakes, gradually beat 185 g sifted icing sugar into 1 egg white, then beat in ¾ teaspoon lemon juice to make a thick, glossy icing. To colour, stir in a couple of drops of food colouring at a time to achieve the desired colour. Spoon onto the cakes, allowing the icing to spread down the domed top in drizzles.

For flat-topped cakes, beat 350 g sifted icing sugar into 2 egg whites, followed by 2½ teaspoons lemon juice to make a thick, glossy icing. To colour, stir in a couple of drops of food colouring at a time to achieve the desired colour. Spoon onto the cakes, allowing the icing to spread to the edges of the paper case and settle in a glossy, smooth surface.

glacé icing

Put 1½ tablespoons lemon juice in a bowl, then gradually beat in 145 g sifted icing sugar to achieve a smooth, spoonable consistency. If necessary, add a drop more lemon juice or a little more icing sugar. To colour, simply beat in a few drops of food colouring until you achieve the desired colour.

chocolate ganache

Put 100 g chopped dark chocolate in a heatproof bowl. Heat 100 ml double cream in a saucepan until almost boiling, then pour it over the chocolate and leave to stand for 5 minutes. Stir the chocolate and cream together until smooth. Leave to cool for 30–60 minutes until thick and glossy, then spread over the cakes.

cream cheese frosting

Beat 150 g cream cheese, 50 g sifted icing sugar and 2 teaspoons lemon juice together until smooth and creamy. Swirl on top of the cakes.

simple cupcakes

A plateful of these pretty, passion fruit-scented cakes look like a swarm of fluttering butterflies. They remind me of the children's tea parties of my youth, where you were guaranteed to find a batch of butterfly cakes clustered on the tea table.

passion fruit butterfly cakes

3 passion fruit

115 g butter, at room temperature

115 g caster sugar

2 eggs

115 g self-raising flour

1 teaspoon baking powder

to decorate

6 passion fruit

150 g mascarpone

4 tablespoons icing sugar, sifted, plus extra for dusting

a 12 hole muffin tin

makes 12

Preheat the oven to 180°C (350°F) Gas 4, then line the muffin tin with paper cases.

Halve the passion fruit. Scoop the flesh into a sieve set over a bowl. Press with the back of a teaspoon to extract the juice.

Beat the butter and sugar together in a bowl until pale and fluffy, then beat in the eggs, one at a time. Sift the flour and baking powder into the mixture and fold in, then stir in the passion fruit juice.

Spoon the mixture into the paper cases, then bake for about 17 minutes until risen and golden and a skewer inserted in the centre comes out clean. Transfer to a wire rack to cool.

To make the topping, halve the passion fruit and scoop the flesh into a sieve set over a bowl. Press with the back of a teaspoon to extract the juice, then add the mascarpone and icing sugar to the bowl. Mix until smooth and creamy. Cover and chill for about 30 minutes to thicken up.

Slice the top off each cake, then cut each top in half. Spoon a generous dollop of the mascarpone mixture onto each cake, then top with the two halves, setting them at an angle to resemble wings. Dust with icing sugar and serve.

Sweet with coconut and tangy with lime, these golden cakes with their snowy-white, ruffled tops look stunning arranged on a coloured plate. Serve them mid-morning with coffee, mid-afternoon with tea or after dinner as a simple dessert.

creamy coconut cupcakes

90 g butter, at room temperature

25 g creamed coconut

115 g caster sugar

2 eggs

100 g self-raising flour

1 teaspoon baking powder

25 g desiccated coconut

grated zest of 1 lime

2 tablespoons milk

to decorate

150 g cream cheese

50 g icing sugar, sifted

2 teaspoons lime juice

40 g coconut shavings

a 12-hole muffin tin

makes 12

Preheat the oven to 180°C (350°F) Gas 4, then line the muffin tin with paper cases.

Beat the butter, creamed coconut and sugar together in a bowl until pale and fluffy, then beat in the eggs, one at a time. Sift the flour and baking powder into the mixture and fold in, then stir in the desiccated coconut and lime zest, followed by the milk.

Spoon the mixture into the paper cases, then bake for about 17 minutes until risen and golden and a skewer inserted in the centre comes out clean. Transfer to a wire rack to cool.

To decorate, beat the cream cheese, icing sugar and lime juice together in a bowl. Swirl the frosting on top of the cakes, then sprinkle over the coconut shavings in a thick layer.

Warm, nutty and fragrant with orange zest, these light, fluffy, gluten- and dairy-free cakes are plain and simple without being in the least bit dull. They melt in the mouth and are perfect served while still warm from the oven. They're delicious simply dusted with icing sugar, but for those who can't do without a little indulgence, serve them with a dollop of crème fraîche on top.

orange and almond cupcakes

2 eggs
90 g caster sugar
grated zest of 1 orange
80 g ground almonds
3 tablespoons potato flour
about 40 g flaked almonds
icing sugar, for dusting

a 12 hole muffin tin

makes 12

Preheat the oven to 170°C (325°F) Gas 3, then line the muffin tin with paper cases.

Put the eggs and sugar in a bowl and whisk for 5–10 minutes until thick and pale. Add the orange zest, then sift the ground almonds and potato flour into the mixture and fold in.

Spoon the mixture into the paper cases and sprinkle the flaked almonds over the top. Bake for about 22 minutes until risen and golden and a skewer inserted in the centre comes out clean. Transfer to a wire rack and leave to cool slightly before dusting with icing sugar and serving.

Maple syrup and pecans are a classic combination, and no better anywhere than in these light, sticky cakes topped with creamy, buttery frosting and caramelized pecans. Look out for the darker, amber maple syrup as it has a more intense flavour that really shines through in the fluffy, buttery sponge.

maple and pecan cupcakes

115 g butter, at room temperature

50 g soft brown sugar

160 ml maple syrup

2 eggs

115 g self-raising flour

60 g pecan nuts, roughly chopped

to decorate

60 g caster sugar

12 pecan nut halves

50 g butter, at room temperature

3 tablespoons maple syrup

145 g icing sugar, sifted

a 12-hole muffin tin

makes 12

Preheat the oven to 180°C (350°F) Gas 4, then line the muffin tin with paper cases.

Beat the butter and sugar together in a bowl until creamy, then beat in the maple syrup. Beat in the eggs, one at a time, then sift the flour into the mixture and fold in. Fold in the nuts, then spoon the mixture into the paper cases and bake for about 17 minutes until risen and golden and a skewer inserted in the centre comes out clean. Transfer to a wire rack to cool.

To make the caramelized pecans, put the caster sugar in a saucepan and add 2 tablespoons water. Heat gently, stirring, until the sugar melts and dissolves. Increase the heat and boil for about 6 minutes until it turns a pale gold colour. Spread the nuts out on a sheet of greaseproof paper and spoon over a little of the caramel to cover each nut individually. Leave to cool.

Beat the butter, maple syrup and icing sugar together in a bowl until pale and fluffy. Spread the mixture over the cakes and top each one with a caramelized pecan.

These soft, sticky, dark brown cakes are dense and gingery, and delicious drizzled with a simple lemon icing. If you want elegant flat-topped cakes, make them in large cupcake cases, but if you prefer domed cakes with icing drizzling down the sides, make them in regular-sized cases.

gingerbread cupcakes with lemon icing

60 g butter

50 g soft brown sugar

2 tablespoons golden syrup

2 tablespoons black treacle

1 teaspoon ground ginger

80 ml milk

1 egg, beaten

2 pieces of stem ginger in syrup, drained and chopped

115 g self-raising flour

to decorate

2 tablespoons lemon juice

200 g icing sugar, sifted

2–3 pieces of stem ginger in syrup, drained and chopped

a 12-hole muffin tin

makes 12

Preheat the oven to 170°C (325°F) Gas 3, then line the muffin tin with paper cases.

Put the butter, sugar, golden syrup, treacle and ground ginger in a saucepan and heat gently until melted. Remove the pan from the heat and stir in the milk, then beat in the egg and stem ginger.

Sift the flour into the mixture and fold in. Spoon the mixture into the paper cases and bake for about 20 minutes until risen and a skewer inserted in the centre comes out clean. Transfer to a wire rack to cool.

To decorate, pour the lemon juice into a bowl. Gradually sift in the icing sugar, stirring as you go, until smooth, thick and spoonable. Spoon the icing over the cakes and put a few pieces of stem ginger on each one. Leave to set before serving.

100 g soft brown sugar

160 ml sunflower oil

2 eggs

grated zest of 1 orange

seeds from 5 cardamom
pods, crushed

½ teaspoon ground ginger

200 g self-raising flour

2 carrots, grated (about 150 g
grated carrot)

60 g walnuts or pecan nuts,
roughly chopped

to decorate

150 g mascarpone

finely grated zest of 1 orange

1½ teaspoons lemon juice

50 g icing sugar, sifted

a 12-hole muffin tin

makes 12

Lightly spiced and topped with a creamy citrus mascarpone frosting, these delightful little cakes are just the thing when you need a treat. They're not too sweet, but offer just the right combination of crunch, crumble, spice, sweetness and creaminess – plus that little hint of naughtiness that a cupcake should always have.

carrot and cardamom cupcakes

Preheat the oven to 180°C (350°F) Gas 4, then line the muffin tin with paper cases.

Put the sugar in a bowl and break up using the back of a fork, then beat in the oil and eggs. Stir in the orange zest, crushed cardamom seeds and ginger, then sift the flour into the mixture and fold in, followed by the carrots and nuts.

Spoon the mixture into the paper cases and bake for about 20 minutes until risen and a skewer inserted in the centre comes out clean. Transfer to a wire rack to cool.

To decorate, beat the mascarpone, orange zest, lemon juice and icing sugar together in a bowl and spread over the cakes.

Using golden polenta gives these cakes a distinctive texture with an almost crispy bite and a gloriously rich colour. Studded with juicy blueberries and topped with a rich, zesty cream cheese frosting, they offer the perfect pairing of light, fresh fruit and rich, creamy indulgence.

blueberry and lemon cupcakes

50 g polenta

40 g plain flour

1 teaspoon baking powder

1 tablespoon crème fraîche

1½ tablespoons sunflower oil

grated zest of 1 lemon

1 tablespoon lemon juice

1 egg

50 g caster sugar

60 g fresh blueberries

to decorate

150 g cream cheese

100 g icing sugar, sifted

½ teaspoon grated lemon zest

1 tablespoon lemon juice

about 60 g fresh blueberries

strips of lemon zest

a muffin tin

makes 10

Preheat the oven to 180°C (350°F) Gas 4, then line the muffin tin with ten paper cases.

Combine the polenta, flour and baking powder in a bowl, then set aside. Beat the crème fraîche, oil, lemon zest and juice together in a jug, then set aside.

In a separate bowl, whisk the egg and sugar together for about 4 minutes until thick and pale, then add the lemon mixture and fold in. Sift the polenta mixture over the top and fold in to combine.

Spoon the mixture into the paper cases, then drop about 4 blueberries on top of each one, gently pressing them into the mixture. Bake for 15–16 minutes until risen and golden and a skewer inserted in the centre comes out clean. Transfer to a wire rack to cool.

To decorate, beat the cream cheese in a bowl until creamy, then beat in the icing sugar, lemon zest and lemon juice. Swirl big dollops of frosting on top of the cakes and decorate with fresh blueberries and strips of lemon zest.

These rich, dark, chocolatey cakes studded with chocolate-covered coffee beans and topped with a creamy coffee butter frosting are simply divine. Dusted with grated chocolate, they look like a plateful of mini cappuccinos – but don't eat too many or they might keep you awake all night!

choca-mocha cupcakes

100 g dark chocolate

150 g butter, at room temperature

150 g caster sugar

2 eggs

2 tablespoons cocoa powder

100 g self-raising flour

2 teaspoons instant coffee, dissolved in 1 tablespoon boiling water

40 g chocolate-covered coffee beans

to decorate

100 g butter, at room temperature

200 g icing sugar, sifted

2 teaspoons instant coffee, dissolved in 1 tablespoon boiling water

grated dark chocolate

a 12-hole muffin tin

makes 12

Preheat the oven to 180°C (350°F) Gas 4, then line the muffin tin with paper cases.

Melt the chocolate in a heatproof bowl set over a saucepan of simmering water or in a microwave, then set aside to cool.

Beat the butter and sugar together in a bowl until pale and fluffy, then beat in the eggs, one at a time. Stir in the melted chocolate and cocoa powder. Sift the flour into the mixture and stir in, then stir in the dissolved coffee, followed by the coffee beans.

Spoon the mixture into the paper cases and bake for about 20 minutes until risen and a skewer inserted in the centre comes out clean. Transfer to a wire rack to cool.

To decorate, beat the butter, icing sugar and dissolved coffee together in a bowl until pale and fluffy. Spread the mixture smoothly over the cakes and sprinkle with grated chocolate.

Subtly scented with lavender, these golden, buttery cupcakes are deliciously simple with an understated elegance, so they're perfect for serving mid-afternoon with a cup of tea. The fragrant taste of the lavender flowers gives the cakes an elusive hint that you can't quite put your finger on.

lavender cupcakes

115 g caster sugar

¼ teaspoon dried lavender flowers

115 g butter, at room temperature

2 eggs

115 g self-raising flour

2 tablespoons milk

to decorate

185 g icing sugar, sifted

1 egg white

lilac food colouring

12 sprigs of fresh lavender

a 12-hole muffin tin

makes 12

Preheat the oven to 180°C (350°F) Gas 4, then line the muffin tin with paper cases.

Put the sugar and lavender flowers in a food processor and process briefly to combine. Tip the lavender sugar into a bowl with the butter and beat together until pale and fluffy.

Beat the eggs into the butter mixture, one at a time, then sift in the flour and fold in. Stir in the milk, then spoon the mixture into the paper cases. Bake for about 18 minutes until risen and golden and a skewer inserted in the centre comes out clean, then transfer to a wire rack to cool.

To decorate, gradually beat the icing sugar into the egg white in a bowl, then add a few drops of food colouring and stir to achieve a lavender-coloured icing. Spoon the icing over the cakes, then top each one with a sprig of fresh lavender. Leave to set before serving.

Delicately scented with rosewater, these gorgeous pink cupcakes are perfect for girls who like things extra-pretty. I like pale pink sugared rose petals on mine, but darker pink or white will look just as lovely. For an extra indulgence, try stirring 75 g chopped Turkish delight into the cake mixture before spooning it into the paper cases.

rosewater cupcakes

115 g butter, at room temperature

115 g caster sugar

2 eggs

115 g self-raising flour

1 tablespoon rosewater

to decorate

12 pink rose petals

1 egg white, beaten

1 tablespoon caster sugar

1½–2 tablespoons lemon juice

145 g icing sugar

pink food colouring

a 12-hole muffin tin

makes 12

Preheat the oven to 180°C (350°F) Gas 4, then line the muffin tin with paper cases.

Beat the butter and sugar together in a bowl until pale and fluffy, then beat in the eggs, one at a time. Sift the flour into the mixture and fold in, then stir in the rosewater.

Spoon the mixture into the paper cases and bake for about 17 minutes until risen and golden and a skewer inserted in the centre comes out clean. Transfer to a wire rack to cool.

To decorate, brush each rose petal with egg white, then sprinkle with caster sugar and leave to dry for about 1 hour.

Put 1½ tablespoons lemon juice in a bowl, then sift the icing sugar into the bowl and stir until smooth. Add a little more lemon juice as required to make a smooth, spoonable icing. Add one or two drops of food colouring to achieve a pale pink frosting, then drizzle over the cakes. Top each one with a sugared rose petal. Leave to set before serving.

With a subtle pale green to the crumb and a subtle taste of pistachio, these little cupcakes are utterly irresistible and unbelievably girly. (Which is just the way they should be!) To achieve a pale pistachio-coloured icing, use a pale green food colouring if you can find one, adding a little at a time until you achieve just the right shade.

pistachio cupcakes

45 g pistachio nuts

115 g butter, at room temperature

115 g caster sugar

2 eggs

100 g self-raising flour

2 tablespoons milk

to decorate

1 egg white

185 g icing sugar

¼ teaspoon lemon juice

green food colouring

12 pink rice paper roses

a 12-hole muffin tin

makes 12

Preheat the oven to 180°C (350°F) Gas 4, then line the muffin tin with paper cases.

Put the pistachio nuts in a food processor and process until finely ground. Set aside.

Beat the butter and sugar together in a bowl until pale and fluffy, then beat in the eggs, one at a time. Stir in the ground nuts, then sift the flour into the mixture and fold in. Stir in the milk and spoon the mixture into the paper cases. Bake for about 18 minutes until risen and golden and a skewer inserted in the centre comes out clean. Transfer to a wire rack to cool.

To decorate, put the egg white in a bowl and gradually sift over the icing sugar, beating in as you go until thick and glossy, then beat in the lemon juice. The icing should be thick but spoonable.

Add a few drops of food colouring to the icing and beat to make a pale pistachio green icing. Spoon on top of the cakes and top each one with a pink rice paper rose. Leave to set before serving.

celebration cupcakes

Bake a batch of these delightfully flirtatious cakes filled with a zesty lemon cream and fresh raspberries for the one you love, and they'll never have eyes for anyone but you! For that extra special touch, buy a muffin tin with heart-shaped holes and push your regular paper cases into the holes.

raspberry love-heart cupcakes

115 g butter, at room temperature

115 g caster sugar

2 eggs

115 g self-raising flour

grated zest and juice of ½ lemon

to decorate

80 ml crème fraîche

1 tablespoon good-quality lemon curd

60 g fresh raspberries

icing sugar, for dusting

a 12-hole muffin tin

makes 12

Preheat the oven to 180°C (350°F) Gas 4, then line the muffin tin with paper cases.

Beat the butter and sugar together in a bowl until pale and fluffy, then beat in the eggs, one at a time. Sift the flour into the mixture and fold in, then stir in the lemon zest and juice. Spoon the mixture into the paper cases and bake for about 18 minutes until risen and golden and a skewer inserted in the centre comes out clean. Transfer to a wire rack to cool.

To decorate, using a sharp, pointed knife, remove a deep round from the centre of each cake, about 3 cm in diameter. Slice the pointed bit off each piece of cored-out cake so that you are left with a flat round. Using a mini heart-shaped cutter, cut the rounds into heart shapes.

Combine the crème fraîche and lemon curd in a bowl, then fold in the raspberries. Spoon the mixture into the hollowed-out cakes, then top with the hearts. Dust with icing sugar.

These pretty pale blue and silver cupcakes are just the thing to get you in the festive mood. The fragrant, fruity buns are much lighter than traditional Christmas cake. Remember to make the fondant stars the day before to give them time to firm up. If you can't find any blue fondant icing, simply add a few drops of blue food colouring to 100 g white fondant icing and knead to make a pale blue icing.

christmas cupcakes

60 g butter, at room temperature

60 g soft brown sugar

1 egg

grated zest of 1 orange

60 g self-raising flour

1 tablespoon brandy

4 ready-to-eat dried figs, chopped

25 g sultanas

70 g glacé cherries, halved

to decorate

100 g blue ready-to-roll fondant icing

350 g icing sugar, sifted

3 egg whites

2½ teaspoons lemon juice

edible silver balls

edible sparkles

pale blue or silver ribbon (optional)

a mini star-shaped biscuit cutter

a 12-hole muffin tin

makes 12

Make the star decorations the day before you plan to make the cakes. Roll out the fondant icing, then use the biscuit cutter to cut out 12 stars. Set aside and leave to dry overnight.

To make the cakes, preheat the oven to 180°C (350°F) Gas 4, then line the muffin tin with paper cases.

Beat the butter and sugar together in a bowl until creamy. Beat in the egg, a little at a time, then stir in the orange zest. Sift the flour into the mixture and fold in, then stir in the brandy, followed by the dried fruit and glacé cherries.

Spoon the mixture into the paper cases and bake for about 14 minutes until risen and golden and a skewer inserted in the centre comes out clean. Transfer to a wire rack to cool.

To decorate, carefully tie a piece of ribbon in a bow around each cake, if liked. Gradually whisk the icing sugar into two of the egg whites in a bowl until smooth and creamy, then beat in the lemon juice. Spoon the mixture over the cakes and scatter over the silver balls. Leave to firm up slightly.

Place the star decorations on top of the cakes, brush with the remaining beaten egg white and scatter with edible sparkles.

Who wants an old-fashioned tiered wedding cake when you could have a mountain of these pretty white wedding cupcakes instead? I like the full-on white look when it comes to the decorations, but you can add pastel food colouring, flowers or ribbon according to your colour scheme. You can also use different-sized muffin tins to make a variety of sizes.

wedding cupcakes

115 g butter, at room temperature

115 g caster sugar

2 eggs

115 g self-raising flour

1 teaspoon vanilla extract or grated lemon zest

2 tablespoons milk

to decorate

1 egg white

125 g icing sugar, sifted

½ teaspoon lemon juice

white edible flower decorations

white lace or organza ribbon

a 12-hole muffin tin

makes 12

Preheat the oven to 180°C (350°F) Gas 4, then line the muffin tin with paper cases.

Beat the butter and sugar together in a bowl until pale and fluffy, then beat in the eggs, one at a time. Sift the flour into the mixture and fold in, then stir in the vanilla extract or lemon zest and the milk.

Spoon the mixture into the paper cases and bake for about 18 minutes until risen and golden and a skewer inserted in the centre comes out clean. Transfer to a wire rack to cool.

To decorate, carefully tie a piece of ribbon around each cake. Put the egg white in a large bowl, then beat in the icing sugar until thick and creamy. Beat in the lemon juice to make a thick, spoonable icing. (If necessary, add a drizzle more lemon juice or a little more sugar to get the right consistency.)

Spoon the icing onto the cakes, then top each one with a flower. The icing hardens quite fast, so work quickly as soon as you've made the icing.

Sweet, spicy pumpkin cakes topped with pretty white and dark chocolate cobwebs are definitely a treat rather than a trick. You can leave the topping to set completely if you like, but they're so much better when the chocolate topping is still soft.

halloween cupcakes

115 g soft brown sugar

120 ml sunflower oil

2 eggs

115 g grated butternut squash or pumpkin

grated zest of 1 lemon

115 g self-raising flour

1 teaspoon baking powder

1 teaspoon ground cinnamon

to decorate

150 g white chocolate, chopped

25 g dark chocolate

a 12-hole muffin tin

makes 12

Preheat the oven to 180°C (350°F) Gas 4, then line the muffin tin with paper cases.

Put the sugar in a bowl and break up with the back of a fork, then beat in the oil and eggs. Fold in the grated squash or pumpkin and lemon zest. Combine the flour, baking powder and cinnamon in a bowl, then sift into the cake mixture and fold in.

Spoon the mixture into the paper cases and bake for about 18 minutes until risen and a skewer inserted in the centre comes out clean. Transfer to a wire rack to cool.

To decorate, put the white and dark chocolate in two separate heatproof bowls. Melt over a saucepan of simmering water or in a microwave. Leave to cool slightly, then spoon the white chocolate over the cakes.

Cut a large square of greaseproof paper and fold into eighths to make a cone and tape together. Spoon the dark chocolate into the cone and snip the tip off so that you can pipe a thin line of chocolate. Put a dot of chocolate in the centre of each cake, then pipe three concentric circles around the dot.

Using a skewer, draw a line from the central dot to the outside edge of the cake and repeat about eight times all the way round to create a spider's web pattern. Serve while the chocolate is still slightly soft and gooey.

You'll never want a traditional birthday cake again after sampling these gooey, chocolatey and nutty baby brownie cakes. Pile them up on a cake stand or plate and gently press a candle into each one. Turn out the lights, light the candles and voilà!

chocolate brownie birthday cupcakes

75 g dark chocolate, chopped

75 g butter

1 egg

75 g caster sugar

25 g self-raising flour

50 g macadamia nuts, pecan nuts or walnuts, coarsely chopped

twelve mini candles

two mini muffin tins

makes 18

Preheat the oven to 180°C (350°F) Gas 4, then line the mini muffin tins with 18 mini muffin or petit fours cases.

Put the chocolate and butter in a heatproof bowl set over a saucepan of gently simmering water and heat, stirring until melted. Remove from the heat and set aside to cool slightly.

When the mixture has cooled, beat in the egg, then stir in the sugar. Sift the flour into the mixture and fold in, then stir in the nuts. Spoon the mixture into the paper cases and bake for about 17 minutes until the top has turned pale and crackly and is just firm to the touch. Transfer to a wire rack to cool, before serving with a glowing candle in the centre of each one.

These pretty floral cakes are perfect for welcoming in the beginning of spring, the warmer weather and the arrival of spring flowers. You could also offer them as a gift for Mother's Day or Easter. Although you can find plenty of simple sugar flower decorations in most supermarkets, it's worth searching out special kitchen shops that will have a wider selection of more unusual and interesting flowers.

spring flower cupcakes

115 g butter, at room temperature

115 g caster sugar

2 eggs

115 g self-raising flour

1 teaspoon vanilla extract

2 tablespoons milk

to decorate

2 egg whites

350 g icing sugar, sifted

2½ teaspoons lemon juice

green and yellow food colouring

12 sugar spring flowers, such as daffodils or daisies

a 12-hole muffin tin

makes 12

Preheat the oven to 180°C (350°F) Gas 4, then line the muffin tin with paper cases.

Beat the butter and sugar together in a bowl until pale and fluffy, then beat in the eggs, one at a time. Sift the flour into the mixture and fold in, then stir in the vanilla extract and milk. Spoon the mixture into the paper cases and bake for about 15 minutes until risen and golden and a skewer inserted in the centre comes out clean. Transfer to a wire rack to cool.

If any of the cakes have domed above the level of the paper case, gently slice off the top using a serrated knife to create a flat surface.

To decorate, put the egg whites in a bowl and gradually beat in the icing sugar, then the lemon juice to give a thick, glossy, spoonable icing.

Divide the icing between two bowls and tint one with green food colouring and the other with yellow to create pretty, fresh pastel shades. Spoon the icing over the cakes – it should naturally spread to the edges of the paper cases. If any air bubbles appear, gently prick with a cocktail stick, then top each cake with a sugar flower. The icing will firm up and set within 1 hour.

For their sheer cuteness alone, these pastel-coloured mini cupcakes are absolutely irresistible. Bake up a batch as a gift for a new mother to celebrate the arrival of her newborn. The white chocolate topping sets, so they're ideal for packing up in a pretty gift box – and just the treat she'll need to get her through those first few sleepless nights.

vanilla and white chocolate babycakes

60 g butter, at room temperature

60 g caster sugar

1 egg, beaten

60 g self-raising flour

¼ teaspoon vanilla extract

1 tablespoon milk

to decorate

60 g white chocolate, chopped

green food colouring

pink food colouring

15 brightly coloured candies

a 12-hole mini muffin tin or a baking sheet

makes 12

Preheat the oven to 180°C (350°F) Gas 4, then line the muffin tin with petit fours cases. (If you don't have a mini muffin tin, arrange the cases on a baking sheet; the cases should be able to cope with such a small amount of mixture.)

Beat the butter and sugar together in a bowl until pale and fluffy, then beat in the egg, a little at a time. Sift the flour into the mixture and fold in, then stir in the vanilla extract and milk.

Spoon the mixture into the paper cases, then bake for about 15 minutes until risen and golden and the tops spring back when gently pressed. Transfer to a wire rack to cool.

To decorate, divide the chocolate among three heatproof bowls and melt over a saucepan of simmering water or in a microwave. Leave to cool slightly, then stir a couple of drops of green food colouring into one bowl of chocolate and a couple of drops of pink into another. Leave the third bowl of chocolate plain.

Spoon white chocolate over four of the cakes, pink over another four and green over the remaining four, then top each one with a candy. Serve while the chocolate is still soft, or leave to set and package up as a gift.

Whether it's 4th July, Bonfire Night or Bastille Day, these sparkling celebration cakes are just the thing to serve when the night sky is exploding with brightly coloured stars. Take a plate of these dense, moist, citrusy chocolate cakes topped with sparklers outside while you watch the fireworks.

firework cupcakes

115 g plain flour

3 tablespoons cocoa powder

½ teaspoon bicarbonate of soda

50 g caster sugar

120 ml orange juice

grated zest of 1 orange

3 tablespoons sunflower oil

1½ teaspoons white wine vinegar

to decorate

100 g dark chocolate, chopped

100 ml double cream

tiny edible silver balls or stars

12 mini sparklers

a 12-hole muffin tin

makes 12

Preheat the oven to 180°C (350°F) Gas 4, then line the muffin tin with paper cases.

Combine the flour, cocoa, bicarbonate of soda and sugar in a bowl. Sift into a larger bowl and make a well in the centre.

Combine the orange juice and zest, oil and vinegar in jug and pour into the dry ingredients. Quickly stir together until combined, then spoon the mixture into the paper cases. (It should be quite liquid and gooey, so you may find a small ladle useful.)

Bake for about 15 minutes until risen and firm on top and a skewer inserted in the centre comes out clean. Transfer to a wire rack to cool.

To decorate, put the chocolate in a heatproof bowl. Heat the cream in a saucepan until almost boiling, then pour over the chocolate. Leave to stand for about 5 minutes, then stir until smooth and creamy. Leave to cool for 5 10 minutes more until thick and glossy, then spread over the cakes.

Sprinkle the frosted cakes with tiny silver balls or stars and stick a sparkler in the centre of each one. Light the sparklers before serving.

indulgent cupcakes

Topped with a cool, creamy mascarpone topping and golden shards of praline, these little cakes offer a pure taste of heaven. A hint of bitter coffee brings out and enhances the flavour of the nutty praline.

coffee and praline cupcakes

115 g caster sugar

60 g blanched hazelnuts

115 g butter, at room temperature

2 eggs

80 g self-raising flour

1 teaspoon baking powder

2 teaspoons instant coffee, dissolved in 1 tablespoon boiling water

to decorate

60 g caster sugar

40 g blanched hazelnuts, roughly chopped

100 g mascarpone

115 g icing sugar, sifted

1 teaspoon instant coffee, dissolved in ½ tablespoon boiling water

a 12-hole muffin tin

a baking sheet

makes 12

Preheat the oven to 180°C (350°F) Gas 4. Line the muffin tin with paper cases and the baking sheet with greaseproof paper.

Put half the sugar in a dry pan and heat gently, stirring, for about 5 minutes until melted and pale gold. Add the hazelnuts and cook, stirring, for about 1 minute, then pour onto the lined baking sheet and leave to harden for at least 20 minutes.

Break the hardened praline into pieces and place in a food processor, then process until finely ground. Set aside.

Beat the butter and the remaining sugar together in a bowl until pale and fluffy, then beat in the ground praline. Beat in the eggs, one at a time, then sift the flour and baking powder into the mixture and fold in. Stir in the dissolved coffee, then spoon the mixture into the paper cases and bake for about 16 minutes until risen and golden and a skewer inserted in the centre comes out clean. Transfer to a wire rack to cool.

To decorate, put the sugar in a dry pan and heat gently, stirring, for about 5 minutes until melted and pale gold. Add the hazelnuts and cook, stirring, for about 30 seconds, then pour onto the lined baking sheet. Leave to harden for about 20 minutes, then break into small shards.

Beat the mascarpone and icing sugar together in a bowl until smooth and creamy, then stir in the dissolved coffee. Swirl the mixture onto the cakes and decorate with shards of praline.

With a gooey chocolate and hazelnut centre, these luscious cakes are deliciously tender. Stirring chocolate and hazelnut spread into the frosting gives it a wonderfully nutty taste to complement the toasted hazelnuts on top.

gooey chocolate and hazelnut cupcakes

75 g dark chocolate, chopped

100 g butter, at room temperature

100 g caster sugar

2 eggs

25 g blanched hazelnuts, ground

100 g self-raising flour

100 g chocolate and hazelnut spread, such as Nutella

to decorate

100 g dark chocolate, chopped

100 ml double cream

2 tablespoons chocolate and hazelnut spread, such as Nutella

about 25 g blanched hazelnuts, toasted and cut into large pieces

a 12-hole muffin tin

makes 12

Preheat the oven to 180°C (350°F) Gas 4, then line the muffin tin with paper cases.

Melt the chocolate in a heatproof bowl set over a saucepan of simmering water or in the microwave, then set aside to cool.

Beat the butter and sugar together in a bowl until pale and fluffy, then beat in the eggs, one at a time. Stir in the ground hazelnuts, then sift the flour into the mixture and fold in. Stir in the melted chocolate.

Drop ½ heaped tablespoonful of the mixture into each paper case, then flatten and make an indentation in the centre of each dollop of mixture using the back of a teaspoon. Drop a generous dollop of chocolate spread into the centre of each one, then top with the remaining cake mixture. Bake for about 18 minutes until risen and the tops spring back when gently pressed. Transfer to a wire rack to cool.

To decorate, put the chocolate in a heatproof bowl. Heat the cream in a saucepan until almost boiling, then pour over the chocolate and leave to stand for 5 minutes. Stir until smooth and creamy, then stir in the chocolate spread. Leave to cool for about 30 minutes until thick and glossy.

Spread the frosting over the cakes and arrange a cluster of nuts in the centre of each one.

Inspired by the classic banoffee pie, these creamy cakes are simply to die for. The tender, moist banana cakes are packed with nuggets of chewy toffee, then topped with whipped cream, sweet and sticky dulce de leche and fresh banana. If you can't find the Spanish dulce de leche in the supermarket, make your own, following the instructions below.

banoffee cupcakes

60 g butter, at room temperature

70 g soft brown sugar

1 egg

1 ripe banana, mashed

115 g self-raising flour

50 g chewy toffees, chopped

to decorate

180 ml double cream, whipped

3–4 tablespoons dulce de leche

1 banana, sliced

a muffin tin

makes 10

Preheat the oven to 180°C (350°F) Gas 4, then line the muffin tin with ten paper cases.

Beat the butter and sugar together in a bowl until creamy, then beat in the egg, a little at a time. Fold in the mashed banana, then sift the flour into the mixture and fold in, followed by the toffees.

Spoon the mixture into the paper cases and bake for about 16 minutes until risen and a skewer inserted in the centre comes out clean. Transfer to a wire rack to cool.

To decorate, swirl the cream over each of the cakes, then drizzle with a spoonful of dulce de leche and top with slices of banana.

Note Dulce de leche is a sweet, gooey toffee sauce from Spain, which is available from larger supermarkets. If you can't find it, you can make it yourself. Put a sealed can of condensed milk in a saucepan, pour over boiling water to cover and boil for three hours, adding more water as necessary so that the can is always covered. Remove from the pan and leave to cool completely before opening using a can opener. Stir well to make a smooth sauce before spooning over the cakes.

These cupcakes, made using a classic Genoese sponge, are light and creamy and perfect for serving in summer when fresh soft berries are sweet, juicy and in season. Because the sponge contains no fat, the cakes don't keep well, so are best eaten on the day they're made.

fresh fruit cupcakes

2 eggs

60 g caster sugar

1 teaspoon vanilla extract

90 g plain flour

to decorate

180 ml double cream

250 g fresh summer berries, such as strawberries, blueberries, raspberries and redcurrants

icing sugar, for dusting

a 12-hole muffin tin

makes 12

Preheat the oven to 180°C (350°F) Gas 4, then line the muffin tin with paper cases.

Put the eggs and sugar in a large bowl and whisk for about 10 minutes until thick and pale. Add the vanilla extract. Sift the flour into a separate bowl twice, then sift into the egg mixture and fold in.

Spoon the mixture into the paper cases and bake for about 12 minutes until risen and golden and a skewer inserted in the centre comes out clean. Transfer to a wire rack to cool.

To decorate, whip the cream in a bowl until it stands in peaks, then swirl over the cakes. Top with fresh berries, dust with icing sugar and serve immediately.

Golden vanilla sponge topped with a thick layer of creamy vanilla and white chocolate cheesecake and decorated with fresh strawberries is the ultimate treat. These cupcakes are best chilled so that the creamy topping sets – but if you just can't wait, they're equally good while it's still soft. Top each cake with one big, fat, glistening strawberry, or nestle a few halves or tiny ones on top.

strawberry cheesecake cupcakes

115 g butter, at room temperature

115 g caster sugar

2 eggs

115 g self-raising flour

½ teaspoon vanilla extract

2 tablespoons milk

to decorate

175 g white chocolate, chopped

175 g cream cheese

6 tablespoons crème fraîche

1½ teaspoons vanilla extract

6 tablespoons icing sugar, sifted

fresh strawberries

a 12-hole muffin tin

makes 12

Preheat the oven to 180°C (350°F) Gas 4, then line the muffin tin with paper cases.

Beat the butter and sugar together in a bowl until pale and fluffy, then beat in the egg, a little at a time. Sift the flour into the mixture and fold in, then stir in the vanilla extract and milk. Spoon the mixture into the paper cases. Bake for about 10 minutes until risen and golden and a skewer inserted in the centre comes out clean. Transfer to a wire rack to cool.

To decorate, check that none of the cakes have risen above the rim of the paper cases. If any have, carefully slice off the top using a serrated knife to create a flat surface.

Melt the chocolate in a heatproof bowl set over a saucepan of simmering water or in a microwave, then set aside to cool slightly. Beat the cream cheese, crème fraîche, vanilla extract and icing sugar together in a separate bowl, then beat in the melted chocolate.

Smooth the cream cheese mixture over the cakes, up to the rim of the paper cases, then chill for at least 1½ hours until set. Decorate with fresh strawberries and serve.

The combination of chocolate, marshmallows and nuts in these sweet and sticky cakes is a taste of pure indulgence. If you've got a really sweet tooth, sprinkle a few extra mini marshmallows on top along with the nuts and chocolate chips, or if you prefer a more adult version, leave them spread simply with the chocolate topping.

rocky road cupcakes

115 g butter, at room temperature

100 g caster sugar

2 eggs

115 g self-raising flour

3 tablespoons cocoa powder

3 tablespoons milk

25 g white chocolate chips

50 g mini marshmallows

25 g flaked almonds or slivered brazil nuts

to decorate

100 g dark chocolate, chopped

100 ml double cream

25 g flaked almonds or slivered brazil nuts

25 g white chocolate chips

mini marshmallows (optional)

a 12-hole muffin tin

makes 12

Preheat the oven to 180°C (350°F) Gas 4, then line the muffin tin with paper cases.

Beat the butter and sugar together in a bowl until pale and fluffy, then beat in the eggs, one at a time. Sift the flour and cocoa into the mixture and fold in. Stir in the milk, followed by the chocolate chips, marshmallows and nuts.

Spoon the mixture into the paper cases and bake for about 18 minutes until risen and the tops spring back when lightly pressed. Transfer to a wire rack to cool.

Put the chocolate in a heatproof bowl. Heat the cream in a saucepan until almost boiling, then pour over the chocolate and leave to stand for about 5 minutes. Stir until smooth and creamy, then leave to cool for about 30 minutes until thick and glossy.

Spread the chocolate mixture over the cakes and sprinkle with nuts, chocolate chips and marshmallows, if liked.

Sinking your teeth into these golden, buttery cakes with their gooey lemon centre and sticky white Italian meringue frosting is a sheer taste of heaven. Try to find a really good-quality lemon curd for the filling to give these little cakes their really intense, lemony flavour.

lemon meringue cupcakes

115 g butter, at room temperature

100 g caster sugar

2 eggs

115 g self-raising flour

grated zest and juice of 1 lemon

3 tablespoons good-quality lemon curd

to decorate

150 g caster sugar

2 egg whites

a 12-hole muffin tin

a piping bag fitted with a star-shaped nozzle (optional)

makes 12

Preheat the oven to 180°C (350°F) Gas 4, then line the muffin tin with paper cases.

Beat the butter and sugar together in a bowl until pale and fluffy, then beat in the eggs, one at a time. Sift the flour into the mixture and fold in, then stir in the lemon zest and juice.

Spoon a good dollop of the mixture into each paper case and make an indentation in the centre with the back of a teaspoon. Drop in a dollop of lemon curd, then top with the remaining cake mixture.

Bake for about 17 minutes until risen and golden and a skewer inserted in the centre comes out clean. Transfer to a wire rack to cool.

To decorate, put the sugar and egg whites in a bowl and set over a saucepan of simmering water. Whisk constantly for about 5 minutes until the mixture is thick and glossy and stands in peaks. Use a piping bag with a star-shaped nozzle to pipe a whirl onto the top of each cake or swirl the meringue over the cakes using a spoon. The frosting will firm up as the cakes sit, so for a soft meringue, leave to set for at least 30 minutes, and for a firm meringue, leave to set for at least 3 hours.

Inspired by the classic Black Forest gateau, these dinky, crumbly chocolate cakes are studded with sweet, sticky cherries and spiked with kirsch. If you really want to go overboard on indulgence, serve them topped with a dollop of whipped cream as well, and shave over some dark chocolate curls.

black forest cupcakes

90 g dark chocolate, chopped

115 g butter, at room temperature

115 g sugar

2 eggs

2 tablespoons ground almonds

150 g self-raising flour

1 tablespoon cocoa powder

2 tablespoons kirsch

50 g glacé cherries, halved

to decorate

100 g dark chocolate, chopped

100 ml double cream

1 tablespoon kirsch

12 glacé cherries

a 12-hole muffin tin

makes 12

Preheat the oven to 180°C (350°F) Gas 4, then line the muffin tin with paper cases.

Melt the chocolate in a heatproof bowl set over a saucepan of simmering water or in a microwave, then set aside to cool.

Beat the butter and sugar together in a bowl until pale and fluffy, then beat in the eggs, one at a time. Beat in the melted chocolate, then stir in the almonds. Sift the flour and cocoa into the mixture and fold in, then fold in the kirsch, followed by the glacé cherries.

Spoon the mixture into the paper cases and bake for about 20 minutes until a skewer inserted in the centre comes out clean. Transfer to a wire rack to cool.

To decorate, put the chocolate in a heatproof bowl. Heat the cream in a saucepan until almost boiling, then pour over the chocolate and leave to stand for 5 minutes. Stir until smooth and creamy, then stir in the kirsch and leave to cool for about 1 hour until thick and glossy. Spread the frosting over the cakes and top with a glacé cherry.

index